Cool Careers in
PHYSICS

Sally Ride
Science

CONTENTS

Iain

Andrés

Julie

Pupa

Gary

Frances

Timothy

Robert

Craig

Jami

Persis

K.C.

What Do You Want to Be?

Is working in physics one of your goals?

The good news is that there are many different paths leading there. The people who work in physics come from many different backgrounds. They include biophysicists, oceanographers, teachers, geophysicists, atmospheric scientists, materials scientists, science illustrators, and many more.

It's never too soon to think about what you want to be. You probably have lots of things that you like to do—maybe you like doing experiments or drawing pictures. Or maybe you like working with numbers or writing stories.

SALLY RIDE
First American Woman in Space

The women and men you're about to meet found their careers by doing what they love. As you read this book and do the activities, think about what you like doing. Then follow your interests, and see where they take you. You just might find your career, too.

Reach for the stars!

Sally K Ride

ANDRÉS LARRAZA
Naval Postgraduate School

A Grandson Shines

When Andrés Larraza was eight, he asked his grandfather why the sky is blue. His answer? "I don't know!" So Andrés found out for himself how waves of light from the Sun collide with gas molecules in the atmosphere. Since blue light is scattered more than the other colors, we usually see blue sky. Andrés thought that if science answered questions his grandfather couldn't, then it was the subject for him!

Sound Choice

In school, Andrés was fascinated by the way sound waves travel through air and water. That led him to work for the Navy, which uses sound, or sonar, underwater to detect submarines. Sound waves are tricky because they can bounce off objects, such as rocks, and take different paths—longer or shorter—to and from a target. This creates echoes, garbling the underwater picture that sonar gives. The solution? Using a technique called time-reversal acoustics, Andrés records how long it takes each sound wave to arrive at a target. He then transmits the slowest waves again, giving them a head start. The fastest waves follow, playing catch-up. That way, all the waves arrive simultaneously and in focus. Goodbye, echo. Hello, submarine.

Two Concerts, One Room

In one of Andrés' favorite experiments, he started with a room that created lots of echoes. Then he played music from two different composers at the same time. Since Andrés figured out how to focus the sound from each composer, he could prevent the sound waves from interfering with each other. That meant you would hear only Beethoven in one part of the room and only Bach in another. *Bravo*, Andrés!

For years, Andrés has volunteered to do cool science at school assemblies. His son Alec is peeking through the smoke.

An acoustics physicist . . .

studies the behavior of sound waves. Andrés researches how to eliminate interference as sound moves through air and water. Other **acoustics physicists**

- design concert halls for the best sound quality.
- study how whales use sound—singing, grunting, gurgling—to communicate and navigate.
- eliminate noise vibrations that annoy aircraft passengers.
- identify human voices by their acoustic "fingerprint."

Is It 4 U?

Which parts of acoustics interest you most?

- Making observations
- Taking measurements
- Designing experiments
- Solving problems

Discuss with a classmate how you could combine these to study how far whales can communicate underwater using sound.

Did U Know?

The English word *telephone* combines the ancient Greek words for far, *tele*, and for sound, *phone*. Now research the Greek roots of the words *television*, *telegram*, and *telescope*. Far out!

Sounds Like *Jeopardy!*

As a class, create a *Jeopardy!* game about sound. Divide into teams and research such categories as Sound Basics, Human Hearing, Sonar, and Music. Then, teams should

- come up with five questions for their category.
- write each answer on a separate index card.
- write point values on the other side of each card, based on the difficulty of the questions.
- on a wall, tape the cards in a column below the category, with the points showing.

Pick one student to act as host—and hold all the correct answers. Then the rest of the class plays the game. Take turns choosing a category and a point value. The first person to raise a hand and ask the correct question wins the points. Who'll win *Sound Jeopardy*?

Iain Couzin
Princeton University

Creatures Featured

Iain grew up in Scotland, where he collected aphids, ants, and other insects. No dogs or cats? Nope—Iain's brothers were allergic to fur. So Iain spent hours watching, sketching, and wondering about his six-legged pets.

"Insects are sort of alien creatures living among us."

All Together Now

Watching ant colonies inspired Iain Couzin to study why some animals bunch together—like in flocks of birds or schools of fish. Sometimes it's about cooperating. Take fish. Swimming close together means more eyes on the lookout for predators such as sharks. Other times, animals swarm for selfish reasons. Take locusts. In Africa, Iain spent days observing the pests swarm and devour entire fields of crops. Were they cooperating? Hardly! The locusts were chasing and eating each another! When there isn't enough vegetation to eat, Iain says, locusts have to make the best of a bad situation.

Crowd Rules

Iain uses his physics smarts to write algorithms—logical sets of instructions—to understand the complex movements of swarms. He's discovered that locusts' attempts to eat, or escape being eaten by, each other get a swarm going. Iain creates computer simulations that follow his algorithms to mimic swarms. His simulations are used by other scientists. They investigate all kinds of things such as how cancer cells may cooperate in forming tumors or how to program robots to cooperate on hazardous tasks.

An animal behaviorist . . .

observes how animals act and interact to understand why they behave the way they do. Iain researches how and why some animals swarm. Other **animal behaviorists**

☐ lay out nature preserves.

☐ train pet dogs to be obedient.

☐ design enclosures for farm animals.

☐ prepare animals bred in captivity for release in the wild.

Surprise!

When Iain observes animals, he usually discovers something surprising. It's your turn to do some observing.

• Choose a group of animals—fish, birds, insects, or some other—to observe.
• Create a field log and record the location, time of day, and type and number of animals in the group.
• Record your observations of their behavior, as an ongoing narrative, for 10 minutes.

What about their behavior surprised you, and why? Write about it in your field log.

Is It 4 U?

As an animal behaviorist, Iain enjoys

• traveling to other countries to observe animals.
• creating computer simulations that imitate swarms.
• using his knowledge and imagination to make sense of data.

Discuss with a classmate what you would enjoy about being an animal behaviorist.

If You Could Walk with the Animals

You and a team of classmates want to study a group of endangered animals. First you need to request funding. Write a proposal that

• includes the animal you'll study, where it lives, and why it's endangered.
• explains the need for your project and how you'll conduct your study.
• describes the animal's habitat, and includes photos.
• introduces your team.

Pass your proposal on to another team who will review it. Will they agree to fund your project?

"We need a combination of energy sources, from wind and biofuels to nuclear."

JULIE LUNDQUIST

Lawrence Livermore National Laboratory

Blowin' in the Wind

Julie Lundquist was blown away by college! During an internship at the National Center for Atmospheric Research in Colorado, Julie learned firsthand how complex wind can be. Now, her research helps turbines catch the wind to generate electricity. "Wind is a pretty incredible, renewable energy resource," Julie says. Unfortunately, the wind doesn't always blow as steadily as we would like. It's just not that dependable—not like Julie.

Sea Change

Julie now forecasts wind speed and direction hours or days in advance. She studies the landscape, pores over wind measurements, and runs computer wind simulations to create accurate forecasts. Companies use that information to design better wind turbines, find places for new wind farms, and even predict how much electricity each wind turbine will generate once it starts spinning. In places like California, Julie's findings could even push wind farms in new directions—like out to sea. "Offshore," she says, "California has incredible wind resources."

Here and There

The wind is always on the move, blowing this way and that—just ask Julie. She grew up on the move too. Every time her dad's Air Force job took the family somewhere new, however, Julie settled in quickly. What kept her so grounded? A love for learning and her outgoing personality!

When not at work, Julie likes to spend time outdoors.

Atmospheric scientists . . .

study the chemistry, conditions, and behavior of the air that surrounds Earth. Julie creates wind forecasts useful for designing and placing wind turbines. Other **atmospheric scientists**

- ☐ forecast the weather.
- ☐ study clouds and their effects on global warming.
- ☐ create high-altitude wind maps used by airlines.
- ☐ predict rainfall patterns relied on by farmers.

Pedal Power

Julie likes to ride her bicycle with her husband and young son. Her bicycle is a machine, like a wind turbine. Julie's leg muscles transfer energy to move the bicycle's pedals, just like wind transfers energy to push the turbines. Her muscle power is a renewable energy source!

What are some things you do that make you a renewable energy source? Write about them in your About Me Journal.

Scout It Out

You and your team have been hired by Windy Ways Renewable Energy. Your job is to find the best place to build a row of new wind turbines in your community. The turbines must meet three specifications. The turbines

- must be exposed to strong and steady winds.
- can't be blocked by tall buildings, trees, or hills.
- must be far away from homes, schools, and businesses to prevent noise pollution.

As a team, brainstorm a possible location. Then as a class, pool your ideas. Discuss and debate which would be the best location, then choose one. Create an oral presentation for Windy Ways, explaining why your location fulfills all three specifications.

Whale of a Turbine

Some of the biggest wind turbines stand taller than a 30-story building. Each of the three blades on those turbines can stretch 50.5 meters (166 feet). That's longer than two blue whales laid tail-to-tail!

■ PUPA GILBERT
University of Wisconsin

Tough Stuff

Pupa Gilbert has always loved a challenge. A favorite involved discovering why the lining of abalone shells is so amazingly strong. The biomaterial is called mother-of-pearl or nacre—it rhymes with *acre*. Jewelers admire nacre's shiny iridescence. Pupa admires how it resists fracture. Nacre is composed mostly of the brittle mineral aragonite, but it is *3,000 times* tougher! "You can go over it with a truck and not break it," Pupa says.

Light Work

Pupa used a machine called a synchrotron to discover the secret behind nacre's strength. The synchrotron shined a beam of intensely bright light onto a slice of abalone shell. That revealed nacre's microscopic structure—an irregular mosaic of crystals. Pupa thinks the irregularity gives nacre its toughness, since it keeps it from fracturing along neat lines. She is now learning more about how nacre forms. If scientists could copy the process, it might inspire new ceramic materials useful for making sharper knives or harder tools. That's not Pupa's motivation though! "I just like doing basic science," she says. "Understanding how things form and how they work in nature is exciting."

When in Rome

Growing up in Italy, Pupa wanted to be a scientist. After all, her mom was a chemist and her dad was a microbiologist. They had another plan for Pupa— journalist. Pupa resisted by arguing she would be better at *making* discoveries than writing about them. She won!

Pupa shows off Mephisto—an X-ray microscope she developed herself.

A biophysicist . . .

studies the physics of living organisms, including their form and function. Pupa studies the tiny mineral structures that make up teeth, bones, and shells.

Other **biophysicists**

- ◘ study how the brain stores memories.
- ◘ learn how frogs resist freezing temperatures.
- ◘ explore how bats navigate using echolocation.
- ◘ trace how electrical impulses travel along nerves.

Creature Features

Animals produce biominerals such as aragonite and calcite to make parts of their bodies as hard as rock.

With a team, research these animals, and then create a science poster and presentation. Describe and illustrate at least one feature of each animal that is made up of a biomineral, and how it is used by the animal.

- Elephant
- Chicken
- Sea urchin
- Nautilus
- Human
- Coral

Did U Know?

Shellfish, such as oysters and mussels, sometimes put nacre to beautiful use. They secrete it so it surrounds something irritating, such as a grain of sand, caught inside their shells. Eventually, if enough nacre builds up, it forms a natural bead—a shiny pearl!

About You

Pupa grew up and became a scientist, just like her parents. She followed in their footsteps. In your About Me Journal, write about whose footsteps you would like to follow.

Tusky Tee Hee

Q. Why do elephants have ivory tusks?

A. Iron ones would rust!

Check out your answers on page 36.

GARY GLATZMAIER
University of California, Santa Cruz

Compass Confusion

Hold a compass and it points north. But someday it will point south. Why? Deep inside Earth, molten iron churns and generates a massive magnetic field. That magnetic field flips once every few thousand to every few million years. When it next flips, compass needles will point south instead of north. Why the switch? For decades, many scientists worked on the answer to that question. They had a theory, and now we know their theory was right—thanks to Gary Glatzmaier.

Surprise Me

The discovery was an accident. Gary was only trying to explain why Earth still has a magnetic field at all. Why didn't it fade away like the Moon's? So he spent several years writing the computer program to simulate Earth's magnetic core. After running the program on a supercomputer for almost a year, it did its job—and then some. In the simulation, the magnetic field flipped.

"The outer part of the Earth's core is liquid iron and nickel. The flow is what causes the magnetic field."

Field of Dreams

"As a kid in Minnesota, I would go down to the basement and work with magnets. I was always trying to make something levitate," Gary says. He didn't know then that his childhood fascination with magnets would draw him to his career.

While Gary works, his dogs Kapra (left) and Kea keep him company.

A computational physicist . . .

programs computers to reproduce real world phenomena too large, difficult, or dangerous to study directly. Gary models the Earth's magnetic field. Other **computational physicists**

- ☐ recreate the formation of powerful hurricanes.
- ☐ simulate how air flows around airplanes and rockets.
- ☐ model undersea earthquakes that can generate tsunamis.

Mutual Attraction?

Q. Why did the male magnet ask the female magnet on a date?

A. He was attracted to her.

Is It 4 U?

What do you think you have in common with Gary? Do you ever

- play computer games?
- figure out how something works?
- put together models?
- wonder why it's so difficult to forecast the weather?

Share with a partner what skills you have that would make you a good computational physicist, and why.

Does a giant magnet generate Earth's magnetic field? Nope. It's generated by the motion of molten metals in our planet's core.

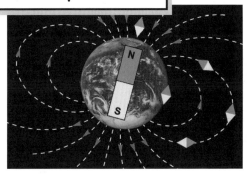

Wandering Poles

Before Earth's magnetic poles completely flip, they wander, or migrate. Between 1831 and 2001, the Magnetic North Pole (MNP) migrated over 1,300 kilometers (808 miles) northward! The table shows the location of the MNP in 2001 (the last year it was measured) and its estimated location from 2002 to 2005. Plot all five locations on a map. Use the map scale to figure out the distance from year to year. Then estimate the MNP's position from 2006 to the present.

Year	Latitude (°N)	Longitude (°W)
2001	81.3	110.8
2002	81.6	111.6
2003	82.0	112.4
2004	82.3	113.4
2005	82.7	114.4

Check out your answers on page 36.

FRANCES HELLMAN
University of California, Berkeley

Physics or Skiing? Maybe Both

Frances Hellman was a nationally ranked ski racer when she was young. She was crazy about sports. But her life took a dramatic turn in high school when she took a physics class. Her teacher showed her that physics was about much more than dry equations. When Frances saw that physics was really about the way the world works at its most basic level—from the reason the Sun shines to the explanation of gravity—she was hooked.

Fun with Magnets!

"I love putting things together and figuring things out," says Frances. That's why she's an experimental physicist—she cooks up new magnetic materials that no one has ever made before. Frances is an expert on magnetism—the attractive force that keeps notes stuck to the refrigerator and compasses pointing north. She hopes to combine the properties of magnetic metals, such as iron, with semiconductors, such as silicon, to make a more powerful computer—one that stores and translates information better and faster than ever.

Still Competitive

Frances is still wild about sports. She skis, but she's also been scoring big on the soccer field. She joined a soccer club in college and has played ever since on a bunch of different teams. In 2004, she was on the team that won the world masters championship for adult athletes. "I was the leading scorer," she says.

"I love playing team sports with other competitive women," says Francis. She's in the back row, fifth from the left.

An experimental physicist . . .

conducts experiments and designs instruments to study everything from subatomic particles to entire galaxies. Frances researches new and exotic materials useful in computers. Other **experimental physicists**

- ☐ design ultrafast trains that glide on magnetic fields.
- ☐ explore young galaxies using space telescopes.
- ☐ create subatomic particles by colliding other particles, such as electrons or protons.

Frances is creative outside her lab too—she made this chandelier!

P.E. Physics

When Frances goes skiing on vacation, she relies on the force of gravity to pull her down the slopes.

- Discuss your favorite sports with a classmate.
- What role does gravity play in each?
- Now, choose one sport and make a presentation to the class, explaining— or demonstrating—how different your sport would be if you played it on the Moon, where gravity is only one-sixth that of Earth's.

Room 4 Improvement

Frances works on creating faster computers. Discuss with a partner a device or tool you use every day— and ways you would like to improve it.

Find Your Way

How does a compass rely on Earth's magnetic field? Find out by making your own. First, ask your teacher for permission and help.

Warning—needles and knives are sharp.

- Magnetize a needle by stroking it in one direction with a magnet.
- Slice off the end of a cork, leaving a small disc.
- Push the needle into the side of the cork disc, through its center. The same amount of needle should stick out of each side.
- Now, float your compass in a bowl of water.

What happens? Why? What happens to your compass if you rotate the bowl?

Check out your answers on page 36.

Tim's been called the U.S. Olympic swim team's secret weapon.

Physics Family Tree

Tim's father and grandfather were both physicists. So, will Tim's career choice rub off on *his* young son and daughter? It's still too early to tell—but they both already swim competitively.

TIMOTHY WEI
Rensselaer Polytechnic Institute

Smooth Move

Tim Wei jokes that he only swims well enough to keep from sinking. So how can Tim help some of the world's fastest swimmers move even faster? It's all about the physics of fluids. Tim is an expert in how fluids such as water and air flow around moving objects. For years, he researched airplanes and ships. Now, you might say, Tim has *pooled* his interests to help the U.S. Olympic swim team.

Know the Flow

To swim faster, Tim says you need to know two things—"how hard you're pushing on the water, and what the water does when you push on it." To find out, Tim videotapes Olympians swimming through sheets of rising bubbles. The way the tiny bubbles flow past their bodies reveals how well swimmers are pushing the water. In one experiment, Tim compared the kick of two swimmers doing the breaststroke. He noticed the first swimmer really pushed the water with her feet, but the second just sliced it. The result? The Olympic coach made sure all his top swimmers got their feet pushing—and not just slicing—to propel them through the water.

Tim and his colleagues set up an experiment with a swimmer.

A fluid dynamicist . . .

studies fluids—liquids and gases—in motion. Tim helps Olympic swimmers adjust their strokes and speed up their movement through the water. Other **fluid dynamicists**

- ◻ analyze how tsunami waves crash against shorelines.
- ◻ design cars that move through the air with little resistance.
- ◻ create computer simulations of how hurricanes evolve.
- ◻ apply their knowledge of how fluid flows to understand traffic and design better roads.

Brain Drain?

Water is much denser than air. That's because its molecules are more closely packed together. A liter of air weighs just 1.25 grams, but a liter of water weighs 1,000 grams or 1 kilogram.

1. Imagine an Olympic-size swimming pool. If the pool holds 1,000,000 liters of water when full, how much does that water weigh in kilograms?
2. Now imagine you have drained the pool. How much does 1,000,000 liters of air weigh in kilograms?

Different Strokes

When you swim, your hands push the water to pull your body forward. Each stroke exerts a force on the water—how much force depends on both the shape and movement of your hands. With a partner, do this investigation and feel the difference for yourself. Fill a tub or big sink with water. Keep a log of what happens when you drag one hand through the water while keeping your fingers

- straight and spread apart.
- straight but joined together.
- joined together and cupped.

Discuss with your partner which position feels like it's pushing the most water around. The least? Which position would you recommend while swimming? Why? As a class, discuss your findings.

Wei's Way?

Tim wanted to work in fluid dynamics "because it's hard." What subject would you choose to study, or what career would you follow, for the challenge?

Check out your answers on page 36.

ROBERT THORNE
Cornell University

Future in the Past

Robert Thorne grew up fascinated with rockets. Even if Robert never rode a rocket to space, his interest *propelled* him into physics. He is now an expert in using X-rays to study the shape of proteins—compounds made by living things that play crucial roles in everything their cells do. So what inspires Robert? "I like to understand how the world works," Robert says—even the ancient world. Robert also uses his X-ray expertise to decipher worn and weathered inscriptions carved in stone 1,800 and more years ago.

Another Blast-off's On!

Growing up in Canada, Robert watched every rocket launch he could on TV. "We all love firecrackers when we're young. These were the biggest firecrackers you could imagine," he says. "The people who designed and built them became my heroes."

Erode Scholar

Robert realized the Latin and Greek inscriptions could still bear traces of the iron chisels and lead paints used to carve and highlight each letter. So he used a powerful X-ray machine to hunt for metallic traces on real inscriptions borrowed from university museums. His technique worked. It highlighted iron and lead atoms bunched in ways that revealed the outlines of even the faintest ancient letters. "We are reading stones inscribed 100 generations ago," Robert says.

On a business trip to Morocco, Robert gets up close with a snake.

A materials physicist . . .

studies how a material's microscopic shape and structure affects its properties. Robert uses high-intensity X-rays to study the atomic structure of proteins, and to decipher ancient inscriptions. Other **materials physicists**

- ☐ engineer plant-based plastic for car parts.
- ☐ design golf clubs that drive the ball farther.
- ☐ create heat-resistant composites to shield spacecraft parts.

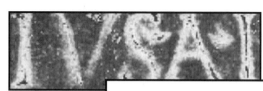

When X-rays zap ancient inscriptions, faded letters are revealed.

Home on the Range

The X-rays that Robert works with are a form of electromagnetic radiation—energy that travels in waves. Microwaves pop popcorn. Radio waves connect cell phones. Scientists classify each type of electromagnetic radiation by how energetic it is. That range, or spectrum, runs from lowest energy to highest energy.

- Research the electromagnetic spectrum.
- Create a science poster with a drawing of the spectrum, labeling the different types of radiation.
- Include examples of how people use the different types of radiation.

Somewhere over ROY G BIV

One very special part of the electromagnetic (EM) spectrum is known by the mnemonic device *ROY G BIV*. Which part of the EM spectrum does this stand for? Why is this part of the EM spectrum so important? When all the waves of light from this part of the EM spectrum are combined, they make white light. Shining white light through a prism, or through water molecules in the air, separates the different wavelengths of light again.

- What do you see when sunlight passes through water vapor in the air?
- Draw your answer.
- Be sure to label it—don't forget ROY G BIV!

Negative Results

Q. Doctor, what does the X-ray of my head show?

A. Absolutely nothing!

Craig loves to go hiking and share nature with his daughter. "I watched a lot of nature specials as a kid."

CRAIG LEE
University of Washington

Marine Machine

Do you think the ocean is just a giant, sloshing saltwater pool? Hardly! Just ask Craig Lee—he follows the action beneath the waves. Craig traces and measures the currents that crisscross the ocean depths and shallows. Some are salty, and some are less so. Some are cold, and some are warm. And sea life? The ocean is Earth's largest ecosystem. More than 80 percent of all living organisms—from seaweed to sharks—live there. Craig studies all of these things.

Sub Substitute

Craig is a diver, but he can't dive every place he studies—like beneath the ice covering the Arctic Ocean. In his place, Craig sends a robotic submarine called a seaglider. The sleek underwater robot measures the differences in water temperature, salinity, and density that drive some currents. On a recent mission, a seaglider tracked fresh Arctic meltwater pouring into the salty Labrador Sea. Global warming could accelerate that melting. That's important to track, Craig says, because it could alter ocean currents—and Earth's climate.

Hands-On, Fins-On

Studying the ocean was a natural choice for Craig—he's loved scuba diving since high school. While in college, Craig even trained researchers to dive in California's Monterey Bay.

Craig is launching a seaglider that will be gathering data for many months.

An oceanographer . . .

studies the composition, structure, and behavior of Earth's oceans. Craig uses small robotic subs to study how fresh water from melting Arctic ice affects ocean current patterns. Other **oceanographers**

- ◻ design deep-diving submarines to explore the ocean's depths.
- ◻ map the shape, or topography, of the ocean floor.
- ◻ discover new species of sea creatures.
- ◻ research communicating underwater using sound waves.

In his spare time, Craig heads up to the mountains.

Rowboat or Rowball?

Team up with a classmate and investigate why objects sink or float.

- Roll a lump of clay into a ball.
- Gently drop the clay into a sink of water. Does it sink or float?
- Remove the clay ball and shape it into a boat. Does it float? If not, tinker with your design until it does.

Discuss your findings, keeping this formula in mind.

$$density = \frac{weight}{volume}$$

Then, write a brief summary of your conclusions and share them with another team.

Is It 4 U?

Which parts of Craig's job would you like?

- Spending time at sea
- Building submarine robots
- Measuring ocean properties, such as saltiness
- Mapping ocean circulation patterns in 3-D

Or is there something else Craig does that interests you? Discuss with a classmate what you would like about being an oceanographer, and why.

Elephunny

Q. How do you make an elephant float?

A. Take an elephant, and add two scoops of ice cream and some root beer!

Check out your answers on page 36.

Jami was the first African-American woman to earn a Ph.D. in physics from Johns Hopkins University.

▪ JAMI VALENTINE
United States Patent and Trademark Office

Up—and a Way

Jami Valentine grew up poor in Philadelphia but enjoyed a rich education. She hatched baby chicks in elementary school and programmed computers in junior high school. In high school, she took summer classes at local colleges. For college, Jami even found a way to go…for *free*! "I realized if you majored in physics, people would give you scholarship money," she says.

Hard-Driven

While attending college in Florida, Jami spent her hot summers doing more cool science! Working alongside top-notch physicists at the Lawrence Livermore National Laboratory in California inspired Jami. It also gave her the confidence to tackle tough questions—such as, how elements with odd names, like gadolinium and dysprosium, could make better computer hard drives. Jami considered becoming a physics professor. Instead, she *reinvented* herself!

Patent Patience

Jami now works as a patent examiner—she analyzes inventions submitted to the U.S. government for review. Jami must decide if each invention is original. If it is, it can be patented—protecting the inventor from copycats. Jami puts her physics know-how to good use, researching transistors and semiconductors, the heart of computers. She reviews hundreds of computer patent applications each year. So far, she has approved just over 80!

Jami shows off a machine that's used to build up the layer-cake design of semiconductors.

A patent examiner. . .

studies new inventions and determines whether they are different enough from other inventions to be patented. Jami analyzes patent applications for computer innovations. Other **patent examiners** focus on new

- ◻ flavors, preservatives, and other food additives.
- ◻ varieties of flowers, crops, fruit trees, and other plants.
- ◻ antibiotics and vaccines.

Cool spectrometers! Jami volunteers to explore science with high schoolers.

Knock-Knock Ha-Ha

Q. Did you hear about the guy who invented the door knocker?

A. He won the *no-bell* prize!

Eureka!

Do you have an idea for an invention you'd like to patent?

- Brainstorm ideas with a classmate. Choose one idea, and then give your invention a title.
- Next, write a one-page description, including how it will be made and used, and who will use it.
- Add a drawing of your invention and label its parts.

Welcome to the club—the U.S. Patent office receives about *500,000* patent applications a year!

Examiners to the Test

After completing the Eureka! activity, decide which team's invention deserves a patent.

- Display the teams' descriptions and drawings.
- Then, as a class, brainstorm five criteria you'll use to judge the inventions.
- Next, each student creates a chart and rates every invention, based on each of the five criteria. Assign a 1–3 value for each criteria, such as creativity—3 equals "good," 2 equals "fair," and 1 equals "poor."
- Pick someone to tally up all the points for each invention.

Which most deserves a patent? It should be *patently* clear!

■ PERSIS DRELL
SLAC National Accelerator Laboratory

Questions That Matter

Persis Drell chases after the smallest of things to answer the biggest of questions. "What's everything made of?" The answer is it's a regular zoo of particles! These particles are the tiniest bits of matter, and have unusual names such as *quark* and *lepton*. Everything, from the biggest mountain to smallest molehill, is made of atoms built from these basic particles. For Persis, studying these particles helps satisfy her curiosity about what makes the Universe go. "I have always been interested in how things work," Persis says.

Bang-up Job

Persis is director of a famous physics lab. It's home to the world's longest linear accelerator. It sends electrons racing down a 3.2-kilometer (2-mile) tube at almost the speed of light to crash into targets. These high-energy collisions produce the particles that particle physicists study.

Dark Mystery

Just as Persis and her colleagues thought they were getting close to really understanding the makeup of the Universe, the Universe threw them a curveball. "We almost had an answer!" Persis says. Instead, physicists were shocked to discover the Universe that we can see—such as planets, stars, and galaxies—makes up only a small portion of what's really out there. Most of the rest of the Universe is invisible dark matter and dark energy. What are they? "We don't know, but we're on their trail," Persis says. "There are lots of questions left to be answered by the next generation of physicists."

Physicists use this accelerator to create high-speed collisions among particles smaller than atoms.

Particle physicists . . .

try to unravel the behavior of the tiniest bits of matter in the Universe. Persis spent years trying to understand just two—the B quark and B meson. Other **particle physicists**

- ◘ collaborate with dozens of other scientists on experiments.
- ◘ design next-generation accelerators.
- ◘ develop hypotheses about dark matter and dark energy.
- ◘ search for new subatomic particles.

Phast Physicists?

Each year, the SLAC National Accelerator Laboratory holds a running race down and back along the length of the linear accelerator. That's a 6.4-kilometer (4-mile) run! Since the first race in 1972, the fastest finish time was about 20 minutes. At that pace, how fast did the winner run in kilometers (miles) per hour? What was the winner's average time per kilometer (mile)?

Chart Your Courses

If you created a bar chart that showed how many men and women there were in Persis' graduate class of 48 students it would look like this.

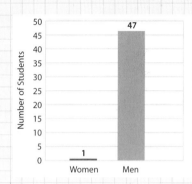

- What percentage of her class were women?
- Next, count the number of girls and boys in your class. Then create your own bar chart.
- What percentage of your class are boys? Girls?

Did U Know?

If we can't see dark matter, how do we know it's there? It still has mass! That mass exerts a force, called gravity, on objects we can see—such as galaxies. So even if we can't see dark matter, we know it's there because of how it tugs on the bright matter we can see.

Check out your answers on page 36.

"I can never stop playing with stuff," says K.C., whose house and office are filled with science toys. **"Play is critical for discovery."**

K.C. COLE

Annenberg School for Communication
University of Southern California

Paid to Play

One of K.C. Cole's first magazine articles was about a scientist who started a nifty science museum called the Exploratorium. "It was just a huge playground with the coolest stuff ever," she says. There were no rules or guards. You could "shrink" yourself or become part of a giant gyroscope. It made K.C. want to be a science writer, so she could write about fascinating stuff all the time. Since then, K.C. has trekked to the top of mountains to observe ultra-powerful telescopes. She's stayed up late with scientists waiting to see if a Mars rover landed safely. "And you actually get paid to do this!" she says.

Girl Talk

K.C. sometimes uses wedding dresses, flowers, and cooking to explain scientific ideas. "If you're going to write about science, you'd better be a pretty writer. Most people don't think they like science because of the dry way it's presented— but they really do."

Far-out Science

K.C. has written eight books and countless articles for newspapers and magazines. Her unique and witty style makes science come to life. It's no wonder her work has been featured in collections of the best of American science writing. K.C. likes writing about physics, especially the weirdest things in the Universe—black holes, time travel, and extra dimensions. "I think it's amazing that real science is so much more far-out than even science fiction," K.C. says.

"The most important thing you can do is to never grow up, to always keep your childlike wonder."

A science writer . . .

explains scientific research and discoveries. K.C. writes articles and books about physics, and teaches science writing. Other **science writers**

- ◻ write for newspapers about the latest science discoveries.
- ◻ create science museum exhibits.
- ◻ publish science books for kids.
- ◻ broadcast science news on TV.

Top 10 Q's

Imagine you're a science writer preparing to interview geophysicist Maria Zuber. First, research what she does and how she works, as well as her interesting background. Next, write a list of professional and personal questions you would like to ask her. Then, share your ideas with your class. Finally, collaborate to create a Top 10 list of interview questions for Maria.

All Good Questions!

"A good science writer is always curious and never afraid to ask questions—even ones they think might be stupid," says K.C. What are you curious about in the natural world?

Figure Newton

An object at rest tends to stay at rest and an object in motion tends to stay in motion unless . . .

from Newton's First Law

All you need to demonstrate Newton's First Law are a few coins.

- First, bend your arm, so your forearm is horizontal and your hand is by your ear. Next, balance a coin on your elbow, as shown.
- Now slowly throw your hand forward and try to catch the quarter. Can you?
- Try flinging your hand faster. What happens?
- Experiment with different speeds until you snatch the coin each time.

Describe what happened, and why. What would Sir Isaac say?

Then, try it again with more than one coin!

Check out your answers on page 36.

About Me

The more you know about yourself, the better you'll be able to plan your future. Start an **About Me Journal** so you can investigate your interests, and scout out your skills and strengths.

Record the date in your journal. Then copy each of the 15 statements below, and write down your responses. Revisit your journal a few times a year to find out how you've changed and grown.

1. *These are things I'd like to do someday.*
   Choose from this list, or create your own.

   - Investigate Earth's atmosphere
   - Design sports equipment
   - Experiment with sound waves
   - Design instruments
   - Understand the physics of how things form
   - Write about science
   - Observe swarms of insects
   - Program computers to run virtual experiments on real phenomena
   - Analyze and review new inventions
   - Study theories of dark matter
   - Use physics to help athletes
   - Use high-intensity X-rays to study ancient writings

2. *These would be part of the perfect job.*
   Choose from this list, or create your own.

   - Public speaking
   - Brainstorming new ideas
   - Working independently
   - Designing a project
   - Writing
   - Using creativity
   - Making things by hand
   - Discussing ideas
   - Teaching
   - Testing hypotheses

3. *These are things that interest me.*
   Here are some of the interests that people in this book had when they were young. They might inspire some ideas for your journal.

   - Painting
   - Collecting insects
   - Working with magnets
   - Skiing in competitions
   - Swimming
   - Watching rocket launches
   - Scuba diving
   - Watching TV nature shows
   - Making discoveries
   - Studying English and physics
   - Programming computers
   - Hiking
   - Sketching insects

4. *These are my favorite subjects in school.*

5. *These are my favorite places to go on field trips.*

6. *These are things I like to investigate in my free time.*

7. *When I work on teams, I like to do this kind of work.*

8. *When I work alone, I like to do this kind of work.*

9. *These are my strengths—in and out of school.*

10. *These things are important to me—in and out of school.*

11. *These are three activities I like to do.*

12. *These are three activities I don't like to do.*

13. *These are three people I admire.*

14. *If I could invite a special guest to school for the day, this is who I'd choose, and why.*

15. *This is my dream career.*

Careers 4 U!

Which career is 4 U?
Physics

What do you need to do to get there? Do some research and ask some questions. Then, take your ideas about your future—plus inspiration from scientists you've read about—and have a blast mapping out your goals.

On paper or poster board, map your plan. Draw three columns labeled **Middle School, High School,** and **College.** Then draw three rows labeled **Classes, Electives,** and **Other Activities.** Now, fill in your future.

Don't hold back—reach for the stars!

Computational Physicist

Astrophysicist

Geophysicist

Physics Professor

Patent Examiner

Planetary Scientist

Science Fiction Writer

Astronomer

Biophysicist

Atmospheric
Scientist

Astronaut

Climate Scientist

Laser Spectroscopy
Scientist

Inventor

Optical Physicist

Physics Lab
Director

Molecular
Physicist

Physics
Teacher

Materials Scientist

Nuclear
Physicist

Animal
Behaviorist

Physicist

Health Physicist

Oceanographer

Systems
Engineer

Journalist

Glossary

aragonite (n.) A mineral similar to calcite, consisting of calcium carbonate ($CaCO_3$) but differing from calcite in its crystallization, density, and less distinct cleavage. (pp. 12, 13)

B meson (n.) Any one of a family of unstable hadrons, also see B quark, made up of a quark and an antiquark. They exist as positive, negative, and neutral particles. (p. 27)

B quark (n.) Any member of the fundamental family of particles from which all hadrons, including protons and neutrons are made. Quarks are held together in hadrons by the strong nuclear force and come in six varieties called flavors. Protons and neutrons are composed of up and down quarks. Heavier quarks called strange, charm, top and bottom quarks are also known. Each flavor of quark has a corresponding antiparticle. (p. 27)

biofuels (n.) Fuels made from renewable resources such as plants or wastes. They replace or reduce the use of fossil fuels such as oil. (p. 10)

calcite (n.) The mineral calcium carbonate, $CaCO_3$. It is the main constituent of limestone, chalk, and marble. (p. 13)

chemistry (n.) The study of the chemical elements and the ways in which they interact with each other. (p. 11)

dark energy (n.) A term used to describe the form of energy that opposes gravity and is thought to be the cause of the Universe expanding and speeding up. (pp. 26, 27)

dark matter (n.) Term used to describe the mass in galaxies and galaxy clusters whose existence is inferred from certain techniques, but has not been confirmed by observations. (pp. 26, 27)

echolocation (n.) A physiological process for locating distant or unseen objects, such as prey, by sound waves reflected back to the emitter, such as a bat, from the objects. (p. 13)

forecast (v.) To calculate or predict some future event or condition, usually as a result of study and analysis of available information. (pp. 10, 11)

gyroscope (n.) System of rotating wheels that allows a spacecraft to maintain a fixed orientation in space. (p. 28)

linear accelerator (n.) A device in which charged particles, such as electrons, are accelerated in a straight line by successive impulses from a series of electric fields. (pp. 26, 27)

magnetic core (n.) The central part of a star or planet. The Earth's core is believed to be composed of nickel and iron, and to be partly liquid with a temperature in excess of 6,000°C. (p.14)

magnetic field (n.) Field that accompanies any electric field and governs the influence of magnetized objects on one another. A small permanent magnet, such as a compass, will tend to turn to point in the direction of the field. (pp. 14, 15, 17)

nacre (n.) The hard pearly substance forming the inner layer of a mollusk shell. (pp. 12, 13)

semiconductors (n.) A material whose electrical conductivity is between that of a conductor and that of an insulator. By far the most important semiconductor is silicon, the material from which many electronic devices, such as integrated circuits, are made. (pp. 16, 24)

sound waves (n.) Longitudinal waves that can be heard by the human ear. Sound waves need to travel through a medium, such as air or water. (pp. 6, 7, 23)

subatomic particle (n.) Particle smaller than the size of an atomic nucleus, including the proton, neutron, and electron, from which atoms are made. (pp. 17, 27)

tsunami (n.) A large ocean wave caused by an underwater earthquake or volcanic eruption. (pp. 15, 19)

wind turbine (n.) A large wheel rotated by the wind to generate electricity. (pp. 10, 11)

Index

CHECK OUT YOUR ANSWERS

BIOPHYSICIST, page 13
Creature Features
Answers may vary.
Elephant: ivory tusks, bones, teeth
Sea urchin: spines
Human: bones, teeth
Chicken: bones, eggshell
Nautilus: shell
Coral: exoskeleton

COMPUTATIONAL PHYSICIST, page 15
Wandering Poles
You might estimate that the MNP will move 30–50 kilometers per year. Below are reasonable estimated locations of the MNP for the years 2006–2010.

Year	Latitude (°N)	Longitude (°W)
2006	83.0	115.2
2007	83.4	116.2
2008	83.7	117.0
2009	84.1	118.0
2010	84.4	118.8

EXPERIMENTAL PHYSICIST, page 17
Find Your Way
When you stroke a needle with a magnet, the action polarizes, or orients, the atoms within the needle in the same direction. When most or all of the atoms in the needle are oriented in the same direction, the needle is magnetized. The magnetized needle should line up with Earth's magnetic field and point to the nearest magnetic pole—north or south. The compass should point in the same direction no matter which way the bowl is turned. Compare to another compass to make sure!

FLUID DYNAMICIST, page 19
Brain Drain?
1. $1{,}000{,}000 \text{ kilograms} = 1{,}000{,}000 \text{ liters} \times \dfrac{1 \text{ kilogram}}{1 \text{ liter}}$

2. $1{,}250 \text{ kilograms}$
$= 1{,}000{,}000 \text{ liters} \times \dfrac{1.25 \text{ grams}}{1 \text{ liter}} \times \dfrac{1 \text{ kilogram}}{1000 \text{ grams}}$

OCEANOGRAPHER, page 23
Rowboat or Rowball
Whether an object will float or sink depends on an object's density compared to the liquid it is immersed in. The clay ball sinks because it is denser than the water it's in. However, if that same clay ball is shaped into a large enough boat, it will float. The weight of the clay is the same, but its volume has increased. This means that the boat's density is less than the density of the clay ball. The formula Density = weight/volume shows this relationship—to make something float you can either reduce its weight or increase its volume.

PHYSICS LABORATORY DIRECTOR, page 27
Phast Physicists?
$19.2 \text{ kilometers per hour} = \dfrac{6.4 \text{ kilometers}}{20 \text{ minutes}} \times \dfrac{60 \text{ minutes}}{1 \text{ hour}}$

$12 \text{ miles per hour} = \dfrac{4 \text{ miles}}{20 \text{ minutes}} \times \dfrac{60 \text{ minutes}}{1 \text{ hour}}$

$\text{Average time is } 3.13 \text{ minutes per kilometer} = \dfrac{20 \text{ minutes}}{6.4 \text{ kilometers}}$

$\text{Average time is } 5 \text{ minutes per mile} = \dfrac{20 \text{ minutes}}{4 \text{ miles}}$

Chart Your Course
$2 \text{ percent women} = \dfrac{1 \text{ woman}}{48 \text{ total students}} \times 100$

SCIENCE WRITER, page 29
Figure Newton
If you fling your hand forward quickly enough, the coin on your elbow will remain at rest just long enough so you can grab it. However, if you throw your hand forward too slowly, the coin will begin to fall to the ground, due to the force of gravity. That doesn't give you time to catch the coin—or impress your friends!

Sally Ride Science is committed to minimizing its environmental impact by using ecologically sound practices. Let's all do our part to create a healthier planet.

These pages are printed on paper made with 100% recycled fiber, 50% post-consumer waste, bleached without chlorine, and manufactured using 100% renewable energy.